T0190991

Game On!

By Maria Le
Illustrations by Clarice Elliott

Ready-to-Read

SIMON SPOTLIGHT
An imprint of Simon & Schuster Children's Publishing Division
New York   London   Toronto   Sydney   New Delhi
1230 Avenue of the Americas, New York, New York 10020
This Simon Spotlight edition August 2024
Text copyright © 2024 by Simon & Schuster, LLC
Illustrations copyright © 2024 by Clarice Elliott
SIMON SPOTLIGHT, READY-TO-READ, and colophon are registered trademarks of Simon & Schuster, LLC.
Simon & Schuster: Celebrating 100 Years of Publishing in 2024
For information about special discounts for bulk purchases, please contact Simon & Schuster Special Sales at
1-866-506-1949 or business@simonandschuster.com.
Manufactured in the United States of America 0724 LAK
2 4 6 8 10 9 7 5 3 1
Library of Congress Cataloging-in-Publication Data
Names: Le, Maria, author. | Elliott, Clarice, illustrator.
Title: Game on! : ready-to-read level 2 / by Maria Le ; illustrations by Clarice Elliott.
Description: New York : Simon Spotlight, 2024. | Series: Ready-to-read. Level 2
Summary: Whether it is basketball, chess, or hopscotch, sports and games bring
people together—and children love to play.
Identifiers: LCCN 2023043073 (print) | LCCN 2023043074 (ebook) | ISBN 9781665957298 (hardcover) |
ISBN 9781665957281 (paperback) | ISBN 9781665957304 (ebook)
Subjects: LCSH: Play—Juvenile literature. | Games—Juvenile literature. | Sports—Juvenile literature. |
CYAC: Play. | Games. | Sports. | LCGFT: Picture books.
Classification: LCC GV182.9 .L4 2024 (print) | LCC GV182.9 (ebook) | DDC 790 [E]—dc23/eng/20240129
LC record available at https://lccn.loc.gov/2023043073
LC ebook record available at https://lccn.loc.gov/2023043074

Glossary

basketball: a court game between two teams where you score points by tossing a ball through the opposing team's raised basket

chess: a board game where two players take turns moving pieces with the goal of cornering the opponent's king piece

cricket: a field game played between two teams that use a ball to try to hit wickets defended by a batter

Deep Blue: an IBM computer that beat the world chess champion after a six-game match

diketo: a game in which a player throws a stone into the air and attempts to grab as many pieces as possible from the ground before catching the falling stone with the same hand

double Dutch: a game in which players jump over two ropes twirling in opposite directions at the same time

football: a field game played between two teams with the aim of moving a ball into the opposing team's goal using any part of the body except for the hands and arms; also known as soccer

grandmaster: an internationally top-rated chess player

hopscotch: a game in which a player tosses an object onto spaces drawn on the ground and hops forward to regain the object

Indigenous: relating to the earliest people known to live in a place

jump rope: a game in which players jump over a twirling rope

mancala: a game in which two players try to win the most pieces by placing and picking up pieces around a board

rock, paper, scissors: a game in which two players form different shapes with their hands and one shape wins out over the other

slam dunk: a shot in basketball made by jumping high into the air and throwing the ball down through the basket

snakes and ladders: a board game in which pictures of snakes and ladders prevent and assist in the players' progress

Note to readers: Some of these words may have more than one definition. The definitions above match how these words are used in this book.

Contents

Chapter 1:
Play Ball!

Let's play ball! All around the world, sports and games bring people together.

Get ready and get set to learn
about the games, sports,
and other activities that kids like
you love to play.

Let's kick off with one of the world's most popular sports: **football**! Some people call this sport "soccer."

In football, players try to score points by moving the ball into the opposite team's goal without using their hands or arms. Instead, players can kick the ball or even use their heads!

Every four years, more than thirty countries around the world compete in a football tournament—the FIFA (say: FEE-fuh) World Cup.

One year the men's teams compete. The next year the women's teams compete.

People all over the globe celebrate and cheer with every goal!

While players kick the ball to score goals in football, points are gained in **basketball** by shooting, or throwing, the ball into the opposite team's basket.

Basketball was invented in the United States. Peach baskets were used in the very first game! When a player scores points by jumping high into the air and throwing the ball down through the basket, it's called a **slam dunk**!

Players kick the ball in football and bounce the ball in basketball. In **cricket**, players hit the ball with a bat!

Cricket is the national sport in England, but it is also popular in Australia, Guyana, India, and Pakistan.
The longest cricket test match in history lasted nine days!

Chapter 2:
Not-So-Boring Board Games!

Not all games involve running, throwing, or jumping.
For some games you only need to use your hands and your brain.

Mancala (say: mahn-KAH-lah) is one of the oldest two-player board games and is played throughout Africa, Asia, and other parts of the world.

Players move playing pieces across the board and then capture them to score points. The player with the most pieces at the end of the game wins.

Chess is a two-player strategy game originating in India. In this game players must think several moves ahead and predict their opponent's moves! Players with extraordinary chess skills are given the title of **grandmaster** by the International Chess Federation.

Humans aren't the only ones that can play chess. You can play chess on a computer, too. In 1997 a chess computer named **Deep Blue** became the first machine to win a match against a grandmaster. Deep Blue won the final game after only nineteen moves!

Board games can challenge your mind and require strategy, calculation, and skill. But some games can be won with just pure luck!

Moksha Patam is an ancient Indian board game that you may now know as **snakes and ladders**!

In this game, players take turns rolling dice and moving their pieces up the gridded board. Be careful!

You might lose your place and slide down a snake. Or maybe luck is on your side and you climb up a ladder to the winning square!

Chapter 3:
On the Playground

Kids all around the world go
to playgrounds to play games!
Some kids like to race across the
playground or chase each other in
a game of tag.

Challenge your speed and skill with
a game of **diketo**, an **Indigenous**
(say: in-DIH-juh-nuss) game from
South Africa.

In this game, players take turns
throwing a rock into the air
and grabbing as many stones
as possible from the ground
before catching the rock
with the same hand.

Hopscotch is a hopping and balancing game. Players must toss an object onto spaces drawn on the ground and jump with one or both feet toward the spot where the object lands. Try not to touch the lines, fall, or lose your balance!

This fun game is played all around the world. In Germany it's called *Hinkspiel*. Croatian players call it *skola*. Among the Igbo in Nigeria it's called *swehi*. In France kids play a spiral version of the game called "escargot," which means "snail"!

Like hopscotch, **jump rope** is another playground activity that requires coordination. Two players hold a rope, one at each end, and twirl the rope in circles. Other players jump over the twirling rope while counting.

You can do single jumps, double jumps, full turns, and even add more jumpers! For double the challenge, twirl two ropes in opposite directions at the same time to play **double Dutch**!

Whether you're on or off
the playground, there's one
game you can play
anytime and anywhere.
It's **rock, paper, scissors**!

Games similar to rock, paper,
scissors are played all across
the world.

In Japan the game is called *janken*. It's called *piedra, papel o tijera* in Mexico. In Indonesia the shapes are not rock, paper, or scissors. Instead they are an ant, a person, and an elephant, and the game is called *semut, orang, gajah*.

From football matches to chess tournaments, sports and games bring people together.

The next time you go to the playground or go out on the field, make some new friends by teaching them all about these fun games from around the world.

Make Your Own Board Game!

Are you ready to play a game you've never played before? It's a game that you'll invent yourself! All you need is the following:

- **adult to help you**
- **large piece of paper**
- **blank note cards**
- **crayons or markers**
- **dice**
- **small toys for game pieces**

Step one: On the large piece of paper, use crayons or markers to draw a path that your game pieces will take throughout the game. Is the path straight or curvy? Are there tricky spots that send players backward or lucky spots that move them forward? Do the colors of the spaces have different meanings?

Step two: On the blank note cards, write some instructions for players to follow during the game. For example, one card can instruct a player to switch spots with another player. A different card can tell a player to move three spaces backward. Make as many different instruction cards as you can!

Step three: Play your board game! Have each player take a turn rolling the dice and moving their game pieces forward. Follow the instructions written on the spaces or the note cards. Whoever reaches the goal first wins!